Black Rose:
Rants, Essays and Letters of an Anarchist

Black Rose:
Rants, Essays and letters of an Anarchist

Abdul Batin Bey

B

Marley Mocha Ink
2016

First Printing: 2016

Marley Mocha Ink
<70B Shrewsbury Green Drive>
Shrewsbury, Ma 01545

AbdulBatinBey@gmail.com

Dedication

To all those who wave the Black Banner

Preface

Hello,

Being an Anarchist is not about being popular or getting votes. Its not about kissing babies (you can if you like) giving long dull speeches that you never intend to live up to, in short its not about pulling the wool over peoples eyes. Anarchy is about being honest with people both in and outside the community. Anarchy is about thinking of new and inventive ways to better the human family not just the corporations and fellow political partiers. Anarchy is also about rebirth and growth and that is what this book is about. As a fellow nonconformist that has been involved in the movement now for almost twenty-three years I thought it was about time to put my pennies on the table. This effort is not meant to slight anyone or to say my vision of the movement should be the only one. Though some of these essays and letters are critical of certain aspects of the modern movement as well as the wider world it is not done with malicious intent but with hopes in trying to move forward out of our current divisive states that the movement as a whole has falling into.

If you are new to the movement I hope this book will get you questioning and searching out all systems that you come across. I hope this book will lead you to a better understanding of the Anarchist movement overall.

If you are a veteran than I hope it helps you too or at the very least give you a new perspective on the topics you will find in this book.

Of course to those who hate Anarchy or the ones who will say I'm not a true Anarchist I hope you at least enjoyed reading the material within.

Peanut Butter and Anarchy: A Free flow of thoughts

Dear Anarchists of the world,

In my years on this earth I have talked to many people and have become a believer in the idea and morals of Anarchy. Though many anarchists give a wide range of different ideas and of different opinions on what Anarchy is the basic tenet is very simple NO BIG GOVERNMENT. The reason for this is because all avenues that incorporate big government from Monarchies, Democracies, Republics and Communism have all ended up the same way that is oppression of the people. Anarchists believe that people would be better off with smaller forms of self-reliance. Also, many Anarchists but not all also believe that money should be taking off the table and that people should do what benefits the human race not out of financial gain but out of betterment for self and others. In some ways Benjamin Franklin did this because most of his inventions he did not patient he let the world have them free of charge. Of course he is not a wholehearted example of Anarchy just that one attribute but I digress.

The first steps have been taking through the Autonomous Zones that the Ravers and certain Anarchists know can work but not forever but I believe that sooner or later Anarchy will have to put into full mode so that its detractors can see how an Anarchist society can work as it has worked in the past.

The first thing we must come to realize is that Anarchy will not rule a nation it is not interested in Nation building so on a grand scale it will fall apart much like socialism. But it can work on a small scale in pockets. So whatever type of Anarchy you believe in you should find others that believe in that same form of Anarchy. Form a society based on your communities' concept of Anarchy. The reason why Anarchists exist in different forms and can exist in different forms is because all forms are seen as a valid expression for instance if some anarchists want to live in a city while others want to go tribal they will not try to force each other to live the way one wants to live they may not agree but respect one another enough to let each other live as they see fit. No other form of Society does that. All others try to force themselves down each other's throats. Anarchists apply this same way of thinking when it comes to religion also. So in a way because of mutual respect the Black Flag community has taking away two of the major reasons of conflict. It is not society or religion in themselves that are the problems but how people treat and react to them.

So far it all sounds Utopian as well as it should considering it is a Utopian Idea. To bring this idea into reality I think we as a whole need to look at some realistic goals. The first realization should be that you would have to give up some comforts of the Capitalistic world because Anarchy demands a simpler way of living. I'm not saying you have to give up on everything but you will have to give up excessive use of electricity, transportation, and your diet will not come from anywhere but in your own back yards. No matter what form of Anarchy downsizing not only o government but also in resources has to come into play. In the long run I think the earth as well as humans health will most likely benefit because we will on some level go back to living a much more ecological existence. We will also live more as a Community, which has tremendous benefits for human health though if you choose to isolate yourself and do everything without human aide except the sweat off of your own back you, can do that if you so desire.

Another realization that flyer of the Black Flag must conclude is that you will not win a war with a government. Meaning you cannot use violence as your way of separating from your oppressors. What I advocate will be an Exodus. All anarchists must ban together for a one-time exodus to a place that they feel they can all share and coexist. Taking the idea of an Autonomous or Squatting to the very real and next logical level. All over the world everyone who believes in Anarchy must shed the shackles of their current oppressors and shout in one voice: Let my people go. Now the governments will struggle and if they attack we have the right to self defense but we should never cast the first stone. To use violence other than selfdefence would be to undo everything we as a community stand for. An exodus is not so much a revolution in the sense of what we have seen but a mere walking away from a bad situation. That which is born in blood she will ultimately be brought down in blood shed.

We should not be interested in bringing anything or anyone down if they don't choose to be. We just want to live life to our choosing as a light to the rest of the world that you can live in an alternate way if you so choose so. Having an anarchist presence even in pockets around the globe will force the rest of the world to become more civil than we are seeing currently. Ounce we leave the world of horror we must always maintain a self-defense mode but never an offensive mode.

Now some might say that I'm advocating a form of military the answer would be yes and no. Your military should be your entire community, I believe that everyone should know how to defend themselves in hopes one never needs to but it would be foolish to never learn how to defend oneself. The no because militaries as we see them in today's world causing harm all over the globe should not exist. Just like a police force should not be needed everyone should know how to handle situations and ban together when are needed. That is the point of an Anarchists Community everyone does there part to help the community stay vibrant. Police officers only exist because most people do not want to take care of themselves so they have to pay people to harass and harm them under the false guise that they are protecting you. No military or police officer has ever aided anyone but themselves they cause people to become violent if people took care of another crime would exist in a very minute form. Everyone would have a task and a roll unfortunately not everyone in our current world has a role and cops make aide the government in keeping certain people down and violent. If you train a dog to be a killer then it will be a killer why would humans be any different? If you push an animal in a corner it will attack why would humans be any different? If you look at how our world operates it wants nothing to do with peace or equality, the reason being if people got along they could not pull the wool over peoples eyes and to them there would be no profit.

The biggest mistake our world currently makes is that materials are more important than individuals. This is why so many people care more about materialistic possession than they do other people. A job sees you as a tool to be used so they can get more materials. Everything is based on empty promises that are not based in reality.

The more you have will not make you any happier because if it did then the rich would not have a higher suicide rate than the poor. It is time that we put individuals back on top that we see each other as valid living beings instead of useless shells that we will use to get what we want then discard when we are done.

Humans must learn to love again. If you humans loved life and felt like they belonged you would not need countries, states, or even rules because you would inherently do what was right. You would help those that needed it when they needed it because there would be no ulterior motive for them to take advantage of you. You would listen to the aged instead of scoffing at them we would ultimate create and achieve what humans have been trying which is Peace on earth.

This ends my free flow and if I need to add or if you want me to add I would be more than happy at another time. I hope that you all enjoyed it and it gave you something to think about.

Your brother in Peace, Love, Truth, Freedom, Justice, and Beauty

Abdul Batin Osman Bey

Revolts

Dear Humans,

I greet you in the name of Peace,

In these days we are seeing revolts happen all over the world, usually through violent methods though there have been a few cases of non-violent revolts. I do support anyone's fight for freedom, as long it's a true revolt by the people for the people. Unfortunately most of these revolts that have happening over the past couple of years have been what I would call false revolt. The reason why I say this is because it seems they are nothing but ploys for the United States to take out those who stand in their way.

One thing all other people around the world should know is that the United States will only help you if you either have what they want or if they want to destroy you both morally and spiritually. The government of the United States has been taking from the majority and turned over to Capitalistic Corporations the president, congress, and all parts of the government are slaves to Businessmen who want to rule the world. As we have seen with most of the middle-eastern countries ounce the revolt happens the United States leaves them in Chaos to die. Why? The United States, which is not a Christian nation though it claims to be, has always seen the Middle East as an enemy both because of its wealth and its adherence to a more simplistic way of life. Capitalism thrives on social disorder and complex way of life. If you don't agree you will be taking down instead of being attacked from without they infiltrated and attack from within. The Middle East is one example of the United States Capitalistic Corporations destruction. They have no real intent in getting rid of so-called Jihad groups unless it serves them to enslave a group of people or to keep the slaves they have happy. Of course many of these Jihad groups are a reaction to the Capitalistic scheme even if they claim otherwise.

Another scheme by these blood thirsty Men of destruction: are that they want people to believe in the idea of Nation Building. The problem with nations is they give a false sense of pride and always lead to Fascist ideals or the concept that some people belong to the Nation more than others and use those undesirables as scapegoats for all there problems which we have all seen or read about both now and in the not too distant past. Capitalism thrives on fascism in fact it causes fascism because it is another form of slavery. The divide and conquer mentality serves the Elite to keep all other people down. This is why special interest groups never help the people they say they are going to help. If you rely on the government then you will always be kept down. The government will only use you to keep the divisions going. This has worked with the false of idea of race for a very long time but due to recent trends this is slowly fading away. Now the satanic government must find new ways to enslave people and if you let them they will.

The only way to have a successful and truly meaningful revolt is to undo the damage that Capitalism has caused. Many people have suggested many ways to do this and they all have valid points. I would say that in order to change the world not only must every nation cease to exist but the idea of separate races must too cease to exist. We are all of one race called the Human Race from the some origin in Sub Sahara Amexem (Africa). In re-establishing this fact I think will greatly alter the course of Human events. We must learn to Love instead of Hate, reclaiming the truth will help the Broken Human family to unite. It will not be an easy over night process only because many people will try to cling and force the idea of many races even though Science proves otherwise. Also they will use skin tone to try to prove their backwards thinking even though every human on earth is a shade of Brown according to science. This must be at the forefront of all revolts. If not then the newly freed people will quickly slide back on old unfortunate habits.

I also see the deindustrialization and a more communal hunter-gatherer ideal of living to be more in tune with the Humans natural way of being. We were made to be gatherers not City Dwellers. This would also mean giving up on some of our more taking for granted comforts and living a more basic lifestyle. If people truly wanted to help the environment they wouldn't make electric cars which actually will cause more harm due to the batteries then any good. Instead they would walk or ride a bike. Taking a few steps back would not only do wonders for the earth but also for human health and dignity since everyone will be participating in the care of one another as the Bedouins and various tribal peoples do. Now I'm not saying all technology should be done away with but we should not rely on technology for every aspect of human life as we currently do.

If not, a hunter-gatherer lifestyle, than a more Voluntary Society, with an Isocratic current. Of course both hunting gathering and Voluntary societies can coexist and overlap. Maybe a form that combines both would be the best solution though it is or has not been fully expressed but the thought is now out in the open for people to build upon.

If you do not have enough people for a full on revolt than start your own Autonomous place and put it into effect. As some of them have tried, succeeded and failed. But the dream must continue until it is realized. It is though these ideals which some would say are Anarchistic (myself included) that ultimate peace will be enjoyed ounce again as it was in our distant past. The current way of life is not and cannot go on. The time to break away from slavery is now because if we don't do it now it may never happen, the window of opportunity is open for but a short time.

I hope you have enjoyed my thoughts.

May you be blessed in all that you do,

Your brother

Abdul Batin Osman Bey

Anarchism in the age of Terrorism

The word Terrorism is thrown around a lot these days and I know many of us shrill at its use because we understand that one mans terrorist is another mans freedom fighter. Having said this I will define terrorist as anyone or group who attacks civilians or innocent people instead of their true enemies the centralized government. Lets be real that is the aim of these groups but instead of attacking in a more straight on way they are doing it through other more circular means. That's the difference between a freedom fighter and a terrorist is that a true freedom fighter goes after those doing the oppression on the masses not attacking the masses in order to get to the oppressor who sees the masses as nothing more than collateral damage though they may mime otherwise with poetic gestures as long as they are relatively safe they really don't care how many innocent people these terrorist kill. That may sound a bit depression to some but it is the obsolete truth.

A question that keeps coming my way is how would an anarchist society deal with such a crisis? Before I begin I would like to point out that as I write this there are anarchist in the middle-east and other parts of the world actually going toe to toe with these terror groups and making more headway than most of our current "Big Brother Savior" countries who seem to be a bit hand tied. To answer the question is not easy since if anarchist did take over they would have to deal with what the Capitalistic world left behind. This may cause Anarchist to take measures they may not have otherwise done if they came into a clean sleight. If Anarchist did take over (either with a clean slate or when they straightened the mess left behind) the first thing that would be hard for terrorist groups is that all centralization would be gone leaving very few areas worth attacking. The entire country would become a huge spider web with lose affiliations here and there but no central buildings, no Olympic size events, no gluttons shopping mauls, all that would be gone no matter what form of Anarchism prevailed. Another factor would be that the police would disappear but everyone would be armed so even if a terrorist did kill or blow something up they would be met with an entire community of armed citizens ready to fire upon them. The reason why terrorism can operate so well is that centralized governments need people unarmed so that they can pretend to defend them though in reality they can do nothing of the sort. In a society were everyone is armed, self-sufficient, and heavily scaled back there would be nothing of strategic value.

A main difference would be that an Anarchist society would pull out of the world economy and the ever-increasing globalization. Terrorism is an exact out come of the meddling of the so-called civilized world forcing its will on other parts of the globe in the name of progress. Anarchists are not going to invade other countries nor will they ally themselves with those who would wish to drag them into wars. Like Sweden Anarchist would allow the world at large to destroy itself as long as they were left in peace. The only way that Anarchist would have to be in a conflict would be in self defense which means the war would have to meet them on their own soil that would always give the Anarchists the home advantage. Now individual Anarchist may fight (as they have in the past) in various causes but an entire society would not be thrown into the jaws of war based on what a few people believe or want. The main reason is that is a form of coercing which is in direct violation of what Anarchists believe.

Some may be wondering about a military the truth is everyone would be the Military in a sense because everyone would be trained to use guns, those who want to learn to fly airplanes would be taught (along with submarines and whatever else is needed) so you would have all the advantages of a Military just not one that is outstanding. The heart of Anarchism is education that encompasses not only the basics of our current education such as Art, Science, English, History, etc but also an education in practical ability of self-reliance like farming, fishing, self-defense in all its forms, and above all the appreciation of life not as something to grudge through like so many people do today but an appreciation to experience every second of life. Since an Anarchist society will not value money, or any commodity over human life, as well as animal life and nature as a whole the value of life will skyrocket and be the way it was many thousands of years ago. Anarchism is the only philosophy that puts life above everything else. Anything that infringes a being from enjoying life is not allowed making them more willing to defend what they have from those who whish to steal it from them.

Terrorism can only exist in world were life is not appreciated but objects and commodity are. As long as countries invade other countries in order to take oil, gold, or simply to impose there will on others you will always have terrorism because you always had terrorism. Terrorism is a natural product of a Capitalistic commodity over life society just like the criminal is a product of the same atmosphere.

Some may read this and say its too idealist too Utopian but that's because they have lived there lives in a corrupt society and Anarchism is a complete opposite of the world we currently dwell in. Anarchism as a whole if one takes the chance to look into it is actually the most practical way of existing that it shunned simply because it is too practical and those with alternative ideas of greed and temporary power do all they can to stop the masses from learning the truth about Anarchism.

Anarchism is not the enemy of the people it is the enemy of those who try to own and control the people.

Anarchist City

One of the main problems within the Anarchist community is that besides the Internet, a few squatters, and various communes hiding either deep in the woods or out in the boondocks there just isn't a visible sign of anywhere. Sure you can read articles, manifestos, read books about what it would be like if we lived in an Anarchist Society, play video games were you can artificially live out the dream but for the vast majority of the populace Anarchism is just a Utopian pie that they either laugh at or simply shrug it off without much thought.

Anarchism as a whole has been giving a pretty bad reputation due to the overwhelming presence of the alternatives. Communist, Socialists, Capitalists, and even Fascists all agree on one topic and that's there hatred for Anarchy. All three have spread lies, rumors, and consider it to be the death nail of civilization. Besides having some great writers and activists who may get in the spot light talking up the merits of Anarchy it has yet to catch on. Even when Anarchists helped various labor parties in the past, joined in civil wars, been beating, lynched, and lord knows what else may have happened the movement is still looked at as a fanatical fantasy that may be alright on paper but would never last in the real world. It is this precise attitude that we need to combat and the easiest way to combat this attitude is to develop our own town and cities. This is the only way that people in the wider population will come to understand the Black Banner.

If Anarchists are not willing to make a visible step forward in a more dramatic way a more noticeable way with the intent of sustainability then what good is being an Anarchist? I know you can point to various communes in the past and even now and talk up how they were brought down by the idiotic governments as some sort of vindication. The truth is even those more known to isolated parts of the world and to freedom fighters are again not known to the public and the ones that do know about them only proves to them that Anarchy has no real merit.

The reason why I entitled this article Anarchist City is because that is a definite way to get people talking, also it would be a place for Anarchists to actually live out there philosophy on a real scale. Communes tend to be small much more easier to contain but a city would give Anarchists every possible pro and con that will allow them to work and grow.

Ina city you have to deal with food, trash, possibly crime, and a whole host of possibilities. In a city without cops for real who will keep the streets clean? Who will farm; mine the stores (if stores even exist) so on and so forth.

Some of these have obvious answers like who will keep the streets clean is easy everybody because everyone will be armed in an Anarchist city. With no authority will people actually pull their own weight or will it simply be flushed down the drain?

Many Anarchists in the past and present had many ideas of how to run an Anarchist Society and how it would spread all over the world creating a better not perfect world. So why not do it? Have a place were there is no authority, no money, no property ownership, individual and communal rights where they are expressed through living them out.

I am one of those Anarchists who believe that it can be done and must be done if the movement is to have any real future. Otherwise the movement will only exist in dream states being nothing more than a mental exercise.

One obstacle that could impede this expedition is the fact that the Anarchist movement is extremely splintered so it might be in the best interest of everyone if the cities were to be declared what sort of Anarchist community they would intend to be that will reduce the amount of in house fighting. Examples would be Anarcho-Communist would have their own City, Anarcho-Sybndalicist, etc etc. I would even suggests that Anarcho- Pacifists to have there own city as well. I know some people belong to more than one school so you would have to decide which one speaks to you more clearly of course if it doesn't pan out you could always leave and try a different Anarchist city. The only ones who I would exempt from this would be the Primitivisms since they don't want to live in a City or town anyways. But all the other forms of Anarchy who talk about forming a society, a brotherhood of man now would be the time to do it.

So come one come all lets build us a city and show these bastards how it is done.

Morality

Some may argue that a society of Anarchists could never be sustained because it appears that those within the movement have an ever-shifting concept of moral law. This couldn't be farther than the truth Anarchist have a very human view of morality namely that morals today may not be morals tomorrow and since humanity is forever growing and learning moral concepts must be able to adapt to these new understandings. Unlike other forms of society Anarchists are true students of both history and human nature whereas they have no misgivings of the constant flux of peoples notions of acceptability.

Having stated the above there have been some constants within Black Rose circles, which I will propose as the foundation (or guidelines) of the society that I believe can best, be applied to all forms of Anarchism.

1. Individuality- people within an anarchist society are responsible for themselves; they have full rights to there own person and can express themselves in and manner that they see fit. Providing that it does not interfere or harm another individual. Actions that violate the sovereignty of any individual are never accepted.

2. Logical Reason- Every aspect of Anarchism is based on a study of science, history, and human nature. Thus when an individual, group, or the society have to make a decision they do based on the logic of that decision. There are no voices calling down from the sky, or assumptions based on emotion.

3. Usefulness or hurtfulness to society- every action is weighed out by how useful or hurtful it is to society. If it were hurtful then it would not be carried out. If it is useful them it will be implemented

4. Treat others and do onto others, as you would like to be treated or have done to you or your loved ones.

The last one may shock people but the majority of Anarchists actually do live by the Golden Rule in a very real way. As I have said before these are the four basic concepts that seem to transcend the lines within the divisions within the movement.

Anarchist society would be exploitive?

I see on many chat forums and political websites the capitalists are trying to say that Anarchy would be more exploitive than Capitalism. This makes me laugh for a couple of reasons the first reason is whenever Capitalists go against Anarchists they always reveal that they do exploit and ruin peoples lives for money and power. They say that fools that will have no compassion for human lives nor have any value of the dollar would run businesses. These Capitalist reveal them and try to say Anarchy is something it is not. Anarchy has no reason to exploit because it is based on the premise that human life and dignity is more important than the almighty dollar. We Anarchists know the value of the dollar but that value is not worth putting our fellow mankind in slavery. The truth is money would be put into its proper place in an Anarchist society if such a society needed money. What threatens the Capitalist is that Anarchists are finding ways around the need for money and false power. People who uphold Capitalism are people who want to have power over other people for personal gain. An Anarchist wants to be equal with everybody knowing that personal happiness will be achieved when everyone is happy. Poverty will vanish because people will not take more than they need just because they can. The Capitalists know that there way of life is coming to an end though they desperately want to cling to it the only option humanity has is to adopt an Anarchist view for the preservation of humanity in the real sense.

Certain aspects would have to be overcome in order for the Anarchist society to work and I am glad that many people inadvertently are taking steps in the right direction. The idea of white privilege must be done away with and will be done away with when no one is physically white of course the mindset may take some time due to the fact that those born with elitist minds may need to be weeded out whether by education or snipping of the balls so they cant breed. The way we think society has to be must be reconsidered, the way we see ourselves and the world must be rethought as well. I would also say we must take a step back from our current position in order to see if the road we are on is actually the right road not just for humanity but for animals as well. If we are to truly be a free society we must undo the Capitalist prison mentality that we are now currently living in.

The Capitalists cannot compete with what others and I are saying nor do they want it to happen. They want war, they want power, and they want to control the masses. I don't think as many egotistical people have lived on earth nurtured by society than our time in history.

Topple Capitalism
Live Anarchy
Live Free

Ziggy says:(one of my black kittens): ;/`erty7 -

Black Rose Lotus: Anarchist Spirituality

It is said that anarchist are not a religious people, on that I would agree. Yet, to say a great deal of anarchists are not spiritual people I would have to disagree in the most severe way. You might find that a queer thing to write but let us look at the differences from an anarchist point of view.

Religion is the dogmatic institution that suffocates the spirit and essence of the true teachings of the prophet, guru, teacher, avatar, and whatever else there might be. Religion as an entity exploits the hopes and fears of the masses for capital gain by creating intolerance towards all those outside of the "inner Circle". To many anarchists religion is the worst part of the Capitalist scheme of control because it comes at you as a sheep though it truly is a wolf. In all my studies I have yet to find one religion that teaches the absolute truth of the book it spouses to be teaching from.

Religion drives obedience and conformity down the throats of every man woman and child that enters its shrines, temples and churches.

Spirituality is for all to believe and grow at there own pace. Dogma is tossed out the window for an open free from restriction experience. In spirituality people may believe or disbelieve what they want, joining or not joining communities that they deem worthy or unworthy. People may use tools or prayers as they wish or use none at all. Every man and woman is a cannon unto himself or herself. Respecting and learning from one another with openness. No one who advocates a spiritual life has to live in fear of what others may do if they have a disagreement with another group of people. Whether one is monotheist or polytheist or whatever the case may be the entire world is big enough to share and to connect with the divine as they see fit. Holy wars and witch hangings will become a permanent thing of the past.

All religions started off as spiritual paths but became corrupted by those who wanted power. By those who wanted the things of this world instead of the benefits of the spirit and this is where the anarchist differs from most people. The anarchist lives a simplistic life; the anarchist shrugs off materialism and extreme excess because the anarchist is a person who learns from the mistakes of both themselves and of others. Unlike the preachers of the world the anarchist does not want to take anything from you, the anarchists do not want you to live in fear of life and of death. No instead they want you to enjoy life and rejoice when death comes knocking at your door and the only that can be done is to embrace the spirit, live as a total community of like minded individuals. To not allow a big Communist capitalist authority but to allow you to be the master of yourself free from the death that religion and current society offers. Salvation cannot be achieved by donations, collection plates; no it can be achieved by actions as well as by embracing the spirit that resides in every living thing.

If you read about any spiritual movement in its infancy they all live in a communal life style. They share food, clothes, daily choirs and daily work. They see and know the struggles of every person and they do not turn anyone who is in need away. Homelessness and unwantedness disappear because every need of every individual is met with the most basic of resources.

What I am writing about can be found in every Holy Book, in every teaching but it seems that only the anarchists whether they believe in a higher power or not are the only ones that cling to these ideals and want to make these ideals a reality for all. Anarchists are not the enemy of God, Avatar, Buddha, or Christ, though many of the religious people who feed off the masses say otherwise. It is the opposed, the anarchist does not seek to destroy religion or society but instead the anarchist seeks to bring religion back to its root the spirit, the essence that will transform society back to its basic simplistic origins.

Live a simple life and you will have more wealth then you ever dreamed of. Treat everyone with respect and you wont have to worry about crime or murder. Spread love to everyone and love will come back to you. Always do the right thing justice will always be done. Tolerate others and others will tolerate you. Create peace to achieve peace. The anarchist spirituality is the rightful spirituality of all creeds and rituals. Man must become what he is taught and knows to be true.

The only paths I see where this anarchist spirituality is achieved is in the Chaos magick, Discordia, and Moorish Orthodox Church, all other paths including various Wicca, Luciferian, and Satanism have all abandoned the spirit for back biting Capitalistic gains of divisions.

So before you join a group or organization ask yourself do they embrace the unity of humanity and encourage the spirit of truth or do they just want to hoodwink you into dogmatic lies.

Conformity

Capitalism has to enforce conformity in order to survive. I would also argue that Communism must use conformity in much the same way. Both systems are based on government control (despite what Communist propagandists say) the only difference is that Capitalism needs to continually grow and spread whereas Communists are happy to be stagnant. Both most definitely need not to be questioned by those it subjects the best way to do this is to have the masses do the majority of controlling for you. Both these systems set up an unrealistic standard of happiness and then watch people attack each other if they do not agree with whatever that standard might be whether it is beauty, money, etc, etc. Also place this standard in so-called entertainment to further ingrain the imaginable standard.

What these system don't understand is that Conformity is why they both fail. Without free thinkers, without individualists, no knew ideas will come into the fold. Everything will slowly cease until it collapses and people wont be able to stop it or think a way out of it because by that time (our time) conformity is such a way of being that to think other than what they have been programmed becomes impossible until the ultimate collapse when people are forced to question what happened and think differently.

If we base our society without any standard of happiness, beauty, wealth or what have you and allow people to be themselves as they are we will most likely see the greatest time in history as far as humanities are concerned which is more important than materialistic items that will be tossed out and decay.

So when our current society falls apart more so than it has done let us take this idea of civilization and remold it into a free individualist community.

Don't believe the lies

In our modern days many Capitalist say they don't look down on there workers and they use terms as "We're all Friends" or You're like family to me" in order to gain a foothold on the minds of those who work for them. The truth is they do look down on you and unfortunately they don't have to be an owner of a company. I'm not saying unfortunately because I think owners have a right to do so but too stress that the evil Capitalist mindset has set its rot so deep in our society that even those who may only be one or two steps above you look down on you. How do I know this? Besides talking to such scum you can tell by body language and tone of voice. Also if you believe the lies that they tell you then question them on there motives and see how quickly they cut you down and show the real them. Yes ladies and gentlemen you are nothing more than a number easily replace with a body whether it be mechanical or flesh.

So why should you the exploited worker obey the minority slave masters? With their lies of economic trickle down that only a fool would believe or with the "We create the jobs" lie that has been disproving numerous times. It is the average person who creates wealth and jobs not the elite. Our current mode of society is based on lie after lie and yet many believe the lie and remain powerless. The majority needs to cast out the minority cancer and start again with a new way of life and looking at one another instead of buying into the false ideals of the Pigs on the Hill. Presidents, politicians won't change unless the people force them to change. Only the majority of people can create a better future and a better world. We have gone as far as the Capitalist ideals can go and they are crumbling all around us in spite of what they are saying.

As humans we have only two choices at hand the first one being that we keep our mouths shut, take no action and remain a silent majority being crushed by the Elite or we can rise up, topple the current system and try a new approach that will lead to a better future for mankind as whole. We are at that point in history it's now or never.

Naturally Greedy

I do not subscribe to any idea that the human is naturally greedy instead I believe it is a taught behavior. The very American notion that people naturally want more, more, and more is complete bogus because when the chips are down people will revert back to there natural instincts which are community and survival. Humans know that they have a better chance at surviving in numbers so they have developed communication skills and a sense of community with one another. The other things which thrives in humans is the need to survive which means if they had to get rid of all there possessions to insure there survival they would do it in a heartbeat as long as they knew the threat was there.

Humans have not needed to survive for a few thousand years now many taking for granted what is now thought of as natural behavior. Society has taking the place of tribe and the need to survive has all but dulled itself into a coma. As the years went by humans where taught that the meaning of life was to be greedy. No other place in the world shows this more than the United States to the point that if you are not greedy then you are a weirdo. Thus the way of the United States is to exploit everyone for your own personal false happiness. Even though everyone knows that the more you have doesn't necessarily make you happy people still chase the dream. A dream that is now landing them in hot water but this trained ideal is ingrained in the majority that they refuse to see what is coming down the line. The complete and utter destruction of all they have ever known. How will these people react in a world that cannot sustain them? When they see everything they have ever acquired turn to dust then what? They will most likely commit suicide either a lone or on a mass level where they bring many down with them.

Those who are prepared for what's to come are those who are already living the correct lifestyle that is a life of simplicity. If you buy only what you need knowing that the extra cushions of life must come second then you will always have more than you need. A greedy lifestyle leads to utter poverty sooner or later. A simple lifestyle leads to a full life forever. The world will only be able to sustain humans when and if they scale down their exasperated ideals of what makes life worthwhile. The hog is about to kick you all off unless you take proper action which is use less waste less. This notion of always needing the next gimmick is not a natural human behavior it is a taught behavior that can no longer be afforded. It is not by accident that the United States does not want the majority of people to know this because the Elite actually believe that they will somehow escape the eventual downfall. Either they will take off to someplace else or be snug and secure behind a gated community. Both these notions are mere illusion but as long as they delude themselves while continuing the culture of greed they will happily watch people destroy themselves.

What Anarchists teach is to return human values to humans themselves by scaling down the wants of society and replacing them with the needs of society. By doing this will humans live as they are suppose to as care takers of themselves, the earth and the animals as well. This is why the Capitalist society deems anarchists as a threat as chaos and as evil. Anarchists want human survival that is compatible with humans natural will. Humans must re teach humans how to be human as strange as it sounds because humans have taught humans how to be inhuman to them selves and to nature. As long as humans keep alive these inhuman ideals we will always have a world of nonstop violence and eco disasters until we blot ourselves out of existence. Stop, scale down, and prolong the life of your species this is the ultimate aim of all anarchists.

Be a humanist
Be an Anarchists
Save the world

Perverts among Anarchists

One of the most disturbing trends that I have seen pop up on various Anarchists forums is various pornographic material depicting under aged children doing sexual things either to other children or to adults. Some of these sites try to down play it by calling it non-nude porn meaning the kids are not naked but they are still striking sexual poses, wearing inappropriate clothing or sucking on penis shaped lollipops. I am not sure who these perverts are or why they have choosing various Anarchists forums to post on. I am also shocked that anyone under the Black Flag would allow child pornography to exist on there site.

I am sure that these perverts would have some sophisticated answer about how they are trying to go against the Capitalist system by taking away false morality. Which is what one expects but the flaw would be very simple to point out and that is pornography especially child pornography is exploitive by its very nature. Even when one done by two consenting adults it is still exploitation because these adults are either being exploited by a corporation or is choosing to exploit themselves for various reasons. To go out find children and then use them for your own sexual pleasure is the most exploitive and damaging thing anyone can do.

Anarchy is against all forced and exploitive actions against the will of another person. Anarchy wants people to grow into who they are not who they have become by a Capitalistic system of demoralization. Child pornography will force these children to become something that they were never meant to be. You are taking away their entire life for your own deviants, which is against the very basis of Anarchy. To believe that Anarchy means to do whatever you want regardless of what happens to others is not Anarchy but Capitalism. It is the Capitalistic system, which has allowed people to think exploiting everything under the sun is good. Pornography thrives in Capitalistic countries because sex is the one thing that Capitalists want to exploit more than anything else. All you weird perverts are doing is exactly what the system wants you to do that is defile yourselves and the minds of the young so that you stay forever a slave to your lower animalistic selves and never gain self control to see the real enemy.

Since you sycophants have made the decision to go against the natural freedoms that the Anarchist advocate you will be punished in one form or another. This is something you degenerates should have thought of before posting your cruel fantasies. Also, the forums that host this will also pay the price. Like many criminals will tell you ounce you harm a child you are lower than scum all true Anarchists agree with this statement because we know it goes against everything that those like us have thrived for. An Anarchist Society is not going to be a child raping Utopia if you believe that it is going to or should be I feel sorry for you when this system is toppled and we Anarchists are in charge.

Anarchy does not want your disgust so Sod off.

The Spirit of the Anarchist

Calling oneself an Anarchist seems more dangerous in our modern enlightened society than ever before. Even the early 1900's had more tolerance for Anarchists then the so-called Liberals and Conservatives of today. One must ask them selves why? Why is the idea of Anarchism so feared? Why does our learned society try to harder and harder to oppress this movement's adherents, art, and literature? The entire culture that Anarchism represents is without question deemed enemy number one. More dangerous than the hippies and other such groups.

The answer is simple, Anarchism represents a society based an absolute freedom to be whom and what you want to be without any slight hint of conformity. Your life is truly in your hands and you will live and die by every decision you make. This is what our conformist society fear. America and other countries of our modern world fear true freedom because if people were truly free the needs of greed would come to an end. True Freedom forces one to value other human life and all life. Capitalism can only exist as long as people are enslaved in mind and in body and unfortunately spirit due to the cowardice's of all the world religions. Our entire system as it stands now is based on misleading people, lies, and pure corruption which is favored by all current politicians, corporations, and greed minded individuals. This is the worst assault on humans in history and the powers of the world are desperately trying to crush those who speak out and fight the system of globalization.

The tighter the enemies of the human world grasp the more apparent they become. We must take a stand now and ask if we are to allow ourselves to become eternal slaves or our own masters. Can we not only destroy the current system but can we destroy the brainwashed mindset we have been forced to take on. Though these thoughts are heavy and need to be answered they must be answered quickly. Wouldn't you want to live in a truly free world without poverty, without wealth, where people simply do what is right because they want to not because they are forced to? These police officers do not help nor do they protect you, no, they are against you. Why is you paying money to those who keep you oppressed and down? They who are suppose to enforce the law act as if they are above the law. The same with judges, politicians, and special interest groups. They should all be removed from power placed on an island and forgotten about.

 If you believe yourself to be free ask yourself am I really free? Or is my so-called freedom just an illusion? Only you should answer for yourself don't keep your life in someone else's hands because they will look out for themselves but they will not look out for you. The military only protects the wealthy they do not protect the poor nor do they protect the middle class. How many rick kids do you see on the front lines? None, because we are nothing but pawns in a game of chess that we are unaware of. Topple the kings and Queens and live as you have never lived before.

Only the deaf and dumb feel safe in conformity and the way of Anarchy is to never conform to somebody else's idea, to never place a crown on anyone else's head except for either God or and imaginable ruler that exists purely in your mind. If you place God as your ruler than you must read and make your own mind up of how God is with you do not let mullah, priest, or rabbi tell you other than what's in your heart and how you perceive the scriptures you read. The imagined ruler you crown should be your own mind.

The spirit of Anarchy is pure freedom; do have what it takes to truly be free?

Capitalists are servants?

As I was listening to the radio the other day I heard the host say that he was a devout Catholic and has always believed in Capitalism because it lives by the teaching of Jesus to serve others. I was shocked considering that what he was saying was the biggest oxymoron anyone could say. Unfortunately he is not the only one trying to use his religious ideologies to sway the masses towards the devils kingdom. These people can't really believe what they are spouting off.

In case people don't know Jesus taught that it is better to serve than to be served and a true person of God should always be a constant servant. The elite Capitalist do not serve anyone except there own greed for power. Capitalist do the opposite of what Jesus said instead they exploit as many as they can and con others into serving them. This same host also said that a person should sweat for their daily bread and be paid fair wages as the Bible says. Again I have to laugh because Capitalist especially those at the top do not sweat but force others to sweat as they reap all the benefits and as far as fair wages no job today pays there employees a fair wage. Instead they pay the people actually doing the work barely livable wages while they take all the excess and live high off the hog.

Capitalism is as anti bible as any system can get because it puts no value on human life but instead on money. It turns some into nothing but disposable tools while others with fat pockets are seen as upstanding citizens. This system is the only system where lunatics run the entire show and the sane people are left out in the cold.

Before you fall for the tricks of the enemies of humanity take a really good look at what Capitalism really has to offer, see what it has really done to humans and ask yourself is this the kind of self centered murderous world that I want my children and children's children to inherit? Or do you want a better way of living a more simplistic way but a way where everyone has only what they need. If so start looking into alternative ways of living and try to implement them, educate people about them and try your best to steer the world in a much more humane society

Healthy Capitalism

Now that the Capitalistic world is starting to crumble its most loyal disciples still will not give it up, instead they are calling for so-called "Healthy Capitalism" in order to get the world back in shape. They are depraved people who admit that Capitalism is based on exploitation and greed but it needs to somehow be a positive greed and a positive exploitation. They will admit that those with all the wealth do absolutely nothing for the betterment of the human condition and leach off the mass populace forcing the middle class to become extinct but they still will not wake up and smell the preverbal coffee.

The point is Capitalism is not nor has it ever been a "Healthy" system the only difference is that people are waking up to the facts. People no longer want to be wage slaves nor do they want to be exploited. The new tactic of these heathens is to say we're in it together, that we all have a part to play when in reality they have no business stealing from the majority of the people what rightly belongs to the people. Trickle down economics is a complete joke the world would be better if we abolished money all together that would be the only "Healthy Choice" that I can see if society is going to continue until then we will see endless misery for the majority while those who offer nothing getting fatter and fatter.

Kill Capitalism

There is no doubt that Capitalism breeds elitism and is supported by white privilege. Almost every white person living in the United States still feels on some level superior to his/her non-white counterpart all because our current society with black president in toe still teach that white is might. This is done not only through economics but emotions as well. The rich and the white buy into the idea that because of skin and wealth they are better than all the rest. Still Capitalism takes it even a step further by having the rich think they are not only above a few but above there own race and law which the system is in full agreement.

We anti-Capitalist must come to the full realization that Capitalism is not only a threat on the political field but also on the mind. We must use the same tactics that the evil ones use to get our side of the story out in the public domain. Everyday they bombard people with images, slogans and ideas that say the more you have the more you hoard the better you are than others that don't have or don't horde. The masses buy into this idea because it's all they see, hear, and feel. These Capitalist are very good at making people feel safe and good while feeding them lies of this is how it must be. The more people that buy into this idea the bigger the government the stronger the power the less freedom people have but people are so brainwashed they cant see themselves as the slaves that they are or have become. Even religious institutions have been side tracked from their true mission by bedding with those individuals who give the biggest donations and neatly place them in their pockets. Capitalism has infiltrated every aspect of society and this is what we must fight every day of our short existence.

It does little to us in these days to tell people how things were when people lived in hunter gatherer societies which up the past four thousand years ago was the way of life and if you did a pie chart it would most likely be the biggest societal wedge. The reason why it does little is because people are too caught up in there gadgets. So then what must we do? We have only two real options, which are:

Option number one: Bloody Revolution

If we are to go down this path of an all out blood bath then we must do it as quick and as concise as possible. Those who must be killed in this revolution will not only be the politicians, certain religious leaders and the big wigs of the corporate world but also those who supported them on Wall Street and they're off spring. Though killing children is abhorred and its something I would not condone if we were to go down the path of past revolts that would have to be a factor. To allow these sons and daughters to live would be completely against the revolution because they would foster hatred to the new way of life and do what they could do avenge there parents deaths. There is no way around this fact, which could be the soul reason the Anarchist Bloody Revolution has not yet happened.

Options number two: Play the game

This means we should buy ad space, have radio programs and open jobs all on Anarchist principles to show people how it could and possibly should be. This way we Anarchists would be a living example of what we are talking about though operating in a Capitalist country would put some strains on how much of our ways we could implement at first I am sure that over time we could get a foot hold in and get more and more on track freeing people from there bondage a few at a time. This is the direction that the current Communists and Socialist have taking and in many ways people are unaware of how much these two ideals have been attached to our collective identity.

If we are to truly rid ourselves of the Capitalistic cancer these are our only two options. One way would be the loss of many lives the other a gradual swaying of the masses. Whatever we decide we must make our decision and act as quick as possible before the current government passes more laws and takes away more freedoms so that we will not have a chance at all to bring peace and love on earth.

Ownership

The idea of ownership has always seemed like a weird idea to me. The notion that we can actually posses something seems to go against every fiber of my being. The earth has existed before humans ever did and will exist long after the human race becomes a memory to our planet. So to actually believe and propagate the twisted concept that we can own chunks of land, minerals, metals, that are freely fiving to us by the earth seems contradictory. Even if we invent or make something we still use the freely giving resources provided for the earth. In our quest of conquest we not only pigeon holed ourselves in a make-believe reality but we are in the process of killing ourselves and depleting the earth of what helps it to exist. If the earth freely gives that why can't we all freely use responsibly? Why must we use not only nature but also each other just to fulfill a greed that amounts to nothing on our deathbeds? Whatever you think you own will one day belong to someone else until it turns to dust or the earth explodes. Nothing, not even us will last or could last forever so to build our lives around a self-destructive lie seems moronic to me.

At one time what I am written was common knowledge back when humans lived simpler lives and were not so consumed by the need to posses. Humans were happy to exist with nature accepting the fact that they are/were apart of nature. Many people today will read what I am writing and most likely either be puzzled because they believe in the lie of progress or they will say who cares and everyone else can go to hell in a hand basket. I am well aware of these types of people so I am writing not only for them but also for like-minded individuals who know what I am saying to be true.

Our social system of money, credit, checks and balances are nothing more than a lie that we keep telling ourselves that is true. Buying selling is simply a dumb way to live yet millions of humans live that way all the time. Those who don't buy into the so-called social norms and don't spend every waking hour consuming are cast aside or made to feel inferior about them. The pack of people do this in hopes that those who see the lie for what it is will conform to the lost majorities views.

Against my better judgment I have choosing to tolerate and live in a society that I not only find absurd but completely lacking humanity. Like other people I am forced to have certain things in order to cope with what I must face everyday. Unlike most other people I feel no attachment to these products and I do my best to avoid buying anything that is not truly needed due to my lack of want or interest in what this society has to offer. Of course it can be difficult navigating among those who are not only taking in by the lie but do there best to become propagators of the lie. They talk about what they own as if it means anything to anyone except himself or herself. I know that no matter how long I live I will never be comfortable in this society or time.

Some may argue that what we have unlike our long distant ancestors is security, which I would argue that they had more security than we ever will. The security they had come by living off the land not pretend money with jobs that mean nothing in the grand scheme of reality. Businessmen, Truck Drivers, Gas Station Attendants, Judgers even Politicians can never have security in a world that is based on illusion as history has proving sooner or later the bubble will burst economics will fail those with the foresight and know how will survive unscathed while those who believe in the social lie will go crazy. Nothing is solid yet so may people believe they are safe and sound never full appreciating that at any second everything they have ever known can come to a complete end.

Unfortunately people can't even turn towards various religious organizations because they too have bought into the profit sharing lie and they need to keep sucking money out of your pockets just like the businessman and tax collector. The very thing that is supposed to guide people away from materialism leads people straight to it. Nothing about any aspect of our society is real it's all false the sooner people wake up and start to go back to basic living the sooner we will have reality and a much more peaceful existence on this small island earth.

Soon we wont even have paper money but credits maybe this will be the lifesaver we need to compound the fact that all we have is a handful of sand. When the mind no longer sees the actual paper and its all on computer based cards maybe then people will finally wake up over throw this fake world and bring it back to reality. Only the utter lazy of body and mind would want this type of society to continue because they could not survive in any other type of social structure. They would be unable to pull there own weight most likely being put out to pasture with all the other corrupt goobers that are happier than pigs in a sty today.

The revolution starts in our minds.

www.ingramcontent.com/pod-product-compliance
Lightning Source LLC
Chambersburg PA
CBHW071140280526
45787CB00003B/1355